Through His Lens

Volume 1

Poetry by Nat Scarcelli

Foreword and Commentaries
by Dina Scarcelli

Oshawa, Canada

2025

Through His Lens: Volume 1
© 2024 by Nat Scarcelli

Reach Nat through Dina Scarcelli at:
Email: dinascarcelli@hotmail.com

ISBN: 978-1-998333-14-1 (Print Book, hardcover) Through His Lens: Volume 1
ISBN: 978-1-998333-13-4 (Print Book, softcover) Through His Lens: Volume 1
ISBN: 978-1-998333-15-8 (E-book) Through His Lens: Volume 1

Published by: Singing Soul Books
Website: www.singingsoulbooks.com
Email: info@singingsoulbooks.com

Disclaimer:
This collection of poems is intended to inspire, provoke thought, and provide moments of reflection. The verses within these pages represent a raw and emotional connection to the world around us, as seen through the lens of the author's personal experiences.

While each poem is deeply personal, readers may find resonance in the words, or simply be moved by the raw emotion conveyed in them. However, the author and publisher assume no responsibility for the interpretation or impact of these poems.
They are offered as reflections of moments, not as solutions.

The beauty of poetry lies in its ability to evoke different emotions and insights for each reader. As such, individual interpretations may vary. Approach these poems with an open heart and mind, allowing them to inspire in ways that are unique to you.

By reading this book, you acknowledge that the journey these poems offer is yours to take—each moment and each word, a reflection of the emotions and thoughts that may unfold as you engage with the poetry. Embrace the journey with an open heart, and let the words guide you in ways that feel right for you.

Table of Contents

Foreword:

The Click of a Moment

My dad always had a passion for photography. The kind of passion that could not be contained by time or place. For him, photography wasn't just about capturing the subject—it was about capturing the essence of a moment, the fleeting emotions that dance through the air at any given time. He would pause, raise his camera to his eye, and with a single click, he would trap that moment in time forever.

His passion wasn't driven by the need for recognition, nor was it tied to technical expertise. It was driven by a personal connection to the world around him. He would stop to photograph a fallen leaf, a dew-covered spiderweb, or a sunset that painted the sky in hues of orange and purple. The beauty he saw was not always the obvious beauty—sometimes it was hidden in the quiet stillness of nature, and sometimes it was in the raw emotion of a passing moment. What mattered was the feeling.

Photography, for him, was about feeling. In every shot, he was not simply capturing an image but preserving an emotion—his own emotion at that specific point in time. He was always in the moment, and when he clicked that shutter, he locked that feeling into the frame for as long as the photograph existed.

Words as a Window to the Soul

Much like his photography, my dad's poetry reflected his emotions at the time of writing. It wasn't something he shared with the world in the conventional sense, but rather, it was a way for him to communicate with those who mattered most—his family, his friends, and sometimes, just himself. He didn't sit down and pen grand verses or perfect rhymes. Instead, his poetry often came in the form of emails—quick, raw, and full of thought.

For my dad, writing was a way of working through his thoughts. Just as he clicked his camera at a moment's notice, he'd type out his feelings when they overwhelmed him. It might be a simple line or a whole series of thoughts that he needed to share, not to gain applause, but to express what was inside. The emails weren't lengthy or polished. They didn't need to be. They were snapshots of his soul, captured in words rather than images.

Each email, each poem, reflected what was going on in his life. It wasn't a matter of impressing anyone, but of connecting. His writing, like his photography, was his way of communicating with the world, with us, even when words might fall short. He may not have spoken often, but when he did, you could hear the weight of his thoughts, the depth of his feelings. The messages were always personal, raw, and sometimes disjointed—but in their disarray, they were beautiful. And to know my dad in the same closeness I do, his words held so much meaning, power, and purpose for anyone who cared enough to read them.

The Heart of His Family

If there is one thing my dad's photography and poetry make clear, it is this: his love for his family is the driving force behind everything he does. These passions aren't separate from his connection to us—they are the means through which he reaches out, expresses love, and captures moments of togetherness. He absolutely loves his family unconditionally. My dad deserves so much, both because of and despite the life he endured.

His photographs may not always include us, but they often represent the places and moments that matter most. They're his silent way of showing us how he sees the world—the world he shares with his family now and the family he once had in the past. Every image he takes now is an expression of how he feels about the world and, indirectly, about the people he loves. Through the lens, he shares his love for the quiet, the beautiful, and the simple moments that fill our lives. The photos he took in the past remind him and us of the love he started to build long ago and of the life he could have ended up with if life had been different.

It is easy to dwell on past events and experiences in life, and through his lens, those were the times he now remembers through old photos that hang all over his walls at his home. Constant reminders of what were and what could have been today if things had been different.

His poetry, too, speaks of this connection. Through his words, he reaches out in ways that go beyond the superficial. He might not always express it in grand gestures, nor can or should he, but his poetry is an intimate window into his soul. His messages often reflect his hopes, his fears, and his gratitude for the people he holds dear. My dad isn't one to boast about his feelings, but if you look closely, you can see them in his photographs and his poetry. The love he has for us, his family, runs deep. And with love, you truly have it all, without having anything at all.

A Different Kind of Connection

In today's world, it's easy to think of connection as something instantaneous and loud—a text, a tweet, a comment, an emoji. But my dad's connection to the world is quieter, more thoughtful, and often indirect. He lives a life of recluse depending on the day. His means of communication may not always align with the fast-paced world we live in, but that's what makes it so special. It's his own way of reaching out, of expressing love and understanding.

While others might seek approval or validation through more conventional means of communication, my dad's approach is different. He's not concerned with being seen by the masses or with fitting into a specific mold. In fact, he is often vocal about his view on the masses. What matters to him is the depth of his connection with the people he cares about. Whether that connection comes through a photograph he took years ago or an email he writes on a quiet evening, he's connecting in his own way. He's choosing to share his world with us, his family, in a way that is deeply personal. For that, I am so grateful.

We may not always understand his approach, but I do. I see him. I understand him. His connection to the world is not measured by likes or comments, but by the way he captures the world through his lens and communicates through his words. Who he is—his essence, his heart—can be found in every image he captures, in every email he sends, in every word he writes. He is a man who would give the shirt off his back to anyone in need, yet he is most in need and always was. Very few truly helped to give him what he needed in his adult life. That saddens me.

Seeing Him Through His Words and Lens

In many ways, this book reflects my dad's life. His photos, his poetry, and his moments of connection with us are a testament to the person he is—a man who doesn't always seek the limelight but is always present, always capturing, always feeling. Through his lens and through his words, we get a glimpse into his soul.

As you read these words, as you see the world through his eyes, I hope you can understand him for even a tiny bit as I do. If you do not, that is okay. I hope that you can read his work and interpret it however it brings you solace.

His immediate family, his photography, and his poetry are all parts of the same whole expressions of a man who feels deeply and loves fiercely. And in a world that often values speed and volume over depth and connection, his way of reaching out is a reminder that the quietest moments (moments he spent in his solitude) are often the most powerful.

This volume of his works was put together with love and honour of one of the most sincere, kindest souls on Earth, who my sister Jennifer and I are so incredibly grateful and blessed to call our dad.

"My dad and I when I was pregnant with my third
and final child, Luke, in 2015."

Through His Lens

Volume 1

ON THE SIDEWALKS OF NORTH YORK

It was no magic carpet ride

Each piece of sidewalk slab

Was a hill

And there were many hills

All in a row as far ahead of me

As my eyes could see.

When it snowed

They were ice capped

Only an avalanche

Or the city plow

Could clear the hills

So I would not slip

And break my neck.

It all came to pass though, without a wow,

Whether hills or torturous mountains

Without heart and empathy,

They all levelled off

And let me be until my time was up

On the sidewalks of North York

By Nat Scarcelli

BY THE SEA

You know by the sea

On that shore

Where we met

A long time ago before…

Before the sea struggled

To be free in front of us

Twisting the water

Into waves

Making noise on the pebbles

Where we stood secure

In our love

The waves were ahead of us

And did not know how

To rise to our hearts

And whisper secrets

They turned back

To the calm

And we would never see them again

To let them know

We broke up!

By Nat Scarcelli

A POEM FOR THE NEEDY

When I was pushing the cart

Over the bridge, one day,

I suddenly realized

What the persistent cold

Was doing to my hands.

It was a sunny day

But as cold as death

It felt like I had no hands.

I could not exercise them

Like my feet

That were always in motion

When I stopped pushing

My hands were frozen in position

Like the one-inch bar of the cart

By which I pushed it around.

Someone bothered to stop

And chat with me the usual way,

Asking stupid questions like the joke of the day.

What's your name? Why are you doing this?

Do you have a home? Where do you live?

And the question of a lifetime,

"Do you need anything????

How can I help you?????"

In those days I had no patience

To answer with the obvious.

I continued my way

In the bitter cold as even the sun

Refused to shine much longer.

Today, my hands are still curled,

As if wrapped around the one-inch bar

In the dead cold.

Stretching them out straight is long forgotten.

Some digits remain curled forever

And deformed.

The moral of the story was and is today, quite simple:

In any economy rationalizing good will to the needy,

If the industrial complex, run by the G7,

Cannot see the problems facing humanity,

For whom are they meeting???

Let them not ask the question of a lifetime,

"How can we help you????"

By Nat Scarcelli

RASCAL

In loving memory of Rascal who lived with me for a little while

I watched Rascal in the back yard

He stared outward to the tall trees in the woods.

I wonder what he saw

And how he saw it.

Would he have, if he could, picked up a pencil
and paper?

And drew the woods?

Would he have noticed the leaves dancing for him?

Would he have cared if the trees reached to
the sky?

And burst the clouds to make some rain?

Would he have felt ambitious enough to chop one down and build a house?

I have spent hours walking with him.

I smelled the scent of the woods oozing from out of the depth of the ravine.

I noticed the beauty of the coloured leaves dangling in every position:

The red against the blue sky or the yellows as vibrant as the sun.

But the dog continued on its way

Sniffing all the spots for who- knows- what.

Without passion.

Not once did he look up to me and say,

"Wow, isn't that a beautiful tree?"

However, the dog kept me company.

The heck with beauty and aesthetics.

His spirit of friendship and companionship was more valuable to me,

than an autumn surge of colours or even a blue bright sky.

By Nat Scarcelli

A POEM FOR US THIS EVENING

They should never be allowed

To stand on their own

In some glorified part of the city,

With trails of blood money

Dripping down from their appetites.

Letting us eat sardines out of a can

(Cold and sterile like their souls),

They should be cut and trimmed

With sharpened knives,

Or tied to posts with firm cement

With chains as long as rainbows

They must never be let free

To nail our innocent hearts to walls,

Or to places where sunlight has a bad effect

And water even worse.

We put them in high places by voting,

But they forget when they get there what to do for us.

They forget on purpose like the story goes

They never weep or cry out loud for us

Nor paint the town in colours that mean life

They forget on purpose and nail us to the wall.

While stealing our wallets and/or purses.

I'd rather hear laughter through the air

And birds coming around

Once in a while to say hello

Or watching curious squirrels looking for a bite to eat,

Or hearing dogs barking crazily to fight off boredom

Or observing sneaky cats prowling the neighbourhood at night

Meowing out loud or snickering at the moonlight.

I'd rather hear the giggling sounds of little children

And grandkids kissing me goodnight

And wishing me love and thanks in a hug and lullaby!

By Nat Scarcelli

MY BIRTHDAY

It sneaked up on me

Even though I knew it would come.

My underwear was too loose, you see,

And my hands raised high, surrendering by the 'sea',

And they fell down around my feet, please don't see.

I became, at that precise moment just another older man,

Sinking slowly to the rocks and sand.

And that's about the size of things to come for all.

So tomorrow, if you are around, just hold my hand,

And for this occasion of just another birthday, all will be grand!

By Nat Scarcelli

Example of an email to explain the above:

"Hello and Good Morning,

I am trying to proofread poems that were written long ago. I sent them at the time as they were written, without proofreading them.

Lately, I've been going over them, and I came across one entitled *MY BIRTHDAY*. It was sent on the last day of December.

This year, in August, I revised it, corrected it, and sent it again. Trouble is, it's not my birthday. My birthday is on the New Year. Hehehe.

The poem is funny because of my trademark imagery, 'underwear tightness.' Hehehe.

Enjoy. I'm trying to make sure, for the sake of Cohen, Dylan, Bukowski, and others, that poetry lives on as a literary format.

Nat"

STREAMING AT TWO O'CLOCK IN THE MORNING

The muscles just don't do

What they're told anymore.

And it's two o'clock in the morning or whatever.

It does not matter anymore:

The time and what is supposed to be done in it.

It could be any time

And you could be dreaming

Or taking a ride for just an hour

From pillow to pillow like on a bus

Or covered with one or two over your head

Like in a subway.

No one cares because they're dead asleep

Dreaming of a different place in staccato beats

Or in fits of light: blended or torn apart,

Or watered or dried out, stained with salty tears.

Egypt comes around and the Sahara

With monuments hanging from the sky

And piles of sand moving at will passed by your windowsill.

You get into your car and wave goodbye to me

You're heading across the Mediterranean

In an outdated boat to places

With chains around their necks, but mountains high around to the sky

To make you feel you are once again free or in love,

Because you sweated and wetted your bed sheets

With a Brady Bunch graduate!

By Nat Scarcelli

"DEAR SUMMER READERS

"I don't know… I write… I don't feel lonely and abandoned when I write… I don't jump on the bandwagon or get bamboozled by the crowds… I write… sometimes just to put ideas into perspective… or to clarify a point of view… or simply to put things in order and make them right in the world… I don't write particularly for children… kids grow up on their own, even though we think we had an almighty hand in child-rearing…

I write when people turn against me or put me in danger or cut off my earnings without warning… I sit down in some corner of my world and write down imagery or ideas… about the bad luck or misfortune or treachery…

I write about backstabbers with long slender knives… or others who know the game and won't share the rules…

I hope you're having a wonderful day wherever you may be… I am here paying the piper, paying the bills, and paying my dues, with a long or short fuse some days.

I speak in tongues in a world of English… it's not the same around the world anymore… The French do not understand the English, and the Germans do not understand the Italians… each nationality sees the world through the eyes of an English language spiced up with Danish,

Norwegian, or even Spanish… eventually, even English will not understand itself around the world… at that point, mankind will climb higher and higher up the Tower of Babel… waiting for the 'final' end of the world… by some spoiled Creator with very tight underwear!

So, whether it's a children's novel or an adult blockbuster with all the elements of fiction or non-fiction, all writing carries a huge label… which is ominously called… a warning.

Good day to all of you…

Good day to Mr. Putin, the Muse of the One Per Cent…"

Nat

Email note between Dad and I:

"Thanks, Dina…

I know homelessness, having spent almost 5 years in that state… mainly the reason my hands and feet are a mess… lol… at the time, who would have thought about today?

There's cold, and then there's cold Arctic style…"

MEETINGS

The waters of the ocean meet the horizon,

Or they meet the ocean shoreline.

The moon climbs high

To meet the clouds and sky.

Even the mountains meet the great blue sky

And pierce the clouds until they rain.

Everything meets something or someone,

Everywhere- there or here.

The summer has no choice but to meet old man winter,

Out of fear with one, two or three tear.

By Nat Scarcelli

Thoughts and funny emails sent from dad, among the pages of emailed poetry:

"CHICKENS AT KFC… grinding the secret ingredients for their flesh… these worker chickens knew nothing of their fate… only the Colonel knew…"

Dad would then insert a free Google image of a flock of chickens turning a mill and slicing a bunch of potatoes, working. He always found a comical image to support his comment.

Sometimes, photos would be attached in the email body with no explanation. However, in the subject line, he would say something that alluded to his thought process, like in this case, where he inserted a free Google image of a homeless man.

"BEFORE ANYONE DARES TO JUDGE ME BY THE TERMS OF CIVILIZATION, KNOW WHERE I CAME FROM ON THE STREETS. OUTSIDE in minus 30 degrees Celsius… NS."

After I commented in a reply email, he wrote:

"Thanks, Dina… I know homelessness, having spent almost 5 years in that state… mainly the reason my hands and feet are a mess… lol… at the time, who would have thought about today? There is cold, and then there is cold Arctic style…"

In another conversation:

"… I will get down to writing one especially for the grandkids (referring to poetry)… but I am still young, still civilized… and warm and alive… and my underwear still gets tight… thanks for the reminders…

I hope all is going well for all of you. I haven't heard from my own family in ages. I don't know what's going on there. Usually, (some) write, but lately, nothing.

You'll get my emails and file them under READ… while time goes into the future and never comes back again."

"FOR: Friends and Family Members (wherever you are)
I am sending you the long version of the poem REMEMBERING…

I hope you remember it as well as you remember me. I need people to remember me once in a while in the same way I remember you in my poetry submissions. Otherwise, why would I send you poetry? I have nothing to gain by doing so monetarily. It's just a way to come to your door. I am only knocking on it and saying, 'Hello.

(Wherever you might be.)
Nat"

REMEMBERING

It was the weather

That changed to its true colour: White!

From the inside it was beautiful

But on the outside

You froze your nuts off

Like leaves in the fall

They felt like falling off.

You must remember the feeling

Those of you who remained male

That awful winter and survived.

The bison out west

Passed by so many times

And not one ever paused to say,

"Isn't the weather lovely this morning?"

Nor did one of them

Ever bring along a paint set

And made a painting of the Rockies

In the middle of a wintery fit.

Only we humans

From another world

Perhaps God's heavenly world

Dared to say how beautiful winter was!

But if you try to remember

The kind of December

When snow was bountiful

And cold did reign.

And if you still remember

You're doing well

And most of all,

You'll know that you're sane.

You'll realize it is coming again.

And it is deadly cold and nasty

If you can remember the truth about it.

So, enjoy the sunshine

And the first days of fall

We're still in September,

And for sure not December!

We'll make it last forever

Because we know what's coming.

An original arrangement by

By Nat Scarcelli

A CHILDHOOD COLD

I could feel the stranger cold

Close to every bone in my body.

It needed my warmth as well,

But there was more of it,

A cold mastermind, a deadly cold,

Unleashed too early in a spell.

When I was a kid, I learned to repel it easier

On an only skating rink outdoors

Playing shinny hockey until midnight

While the arctic air, drifting down from James Bay

To Sudbury, down below, freezing Copper Cliff overnight.

We made our way home when the lights turned off,

Skates still on and steam rising from our bodies

There is nothing like a stranger cold

Close as friendship over your bones.

We made it home though, before the steam froze to ice

There is nothing worse than an ice formation

All over your clothing down to your skin.

You never really get warm until the morning

Just when it's time to walk to school in an Arctic Blizzard.

By Nat Scarcelli

Dad can sketch quite well.

These sketches are illustrations he made based on the poem *"A Childhood Cold."*

Original Pen: Illustrated by Nat Scarcelli

Original pen colourized: Illustrated by Nat Scarcelli

TIME

(Poem one of two with the same title)

Where has the time gone to?

Has it been translated or transformed to another state of existence?

Or even greater sounding, 'dimension'?

Only in memories do I find it

Curled up in a good book

And a couple of great Jpegs by the tens.

I worry about it though; like where did it go?

Did time go through a metamorphosis?

As it did for the Greeks and Romans?

And all the good times have vanished

Forgotten,

Only names appear on rocks and stones!

There's no connection to anyone living or used to live

The stone crumples to the ground

And then what?

It will become a Plains of Abraham in Quebec

But no one on top

Not even one bone to prove existence of humans.

While I am alive and kicking up the dust

I will simply say, A La Mia Famiglia Italiano

Or to all the other Familia's in my repertoire of friends

Merry Christmas, Buon Natale,

And let's go for the dance

While there are ants

In our pants

The Romans danced in Pompeii,

As the lava came rushing out of nowhere

Late at night taking 3D Jpegs overnight.

While the pain floats around

From one place to another

Or something invisible barks against our fragile body

Merry Christmas!

By Nat Scarcelli

BILLS

Realities start their journey to my door.

They announce their approach before the stairs,

And when they get over their shyness,

They start to knock hard against the door.

I have to answer; I've been trained for years

To answer the bloody door and do something.

It is like the old-fashioned telephone call –

I just have to pick it up

When it starts to nervously ring.

I answer it,

In my favorite track pants

And unkept grooming,

I find them at an open door,

Completely ahead of time.

A rehearsal, I guess, a false alarm so I shut the door.

And I think nothing of it the whole day through.

But the guests at the door were not stupid

Or out of touch.

They'll be back when I least expect it.

They know where I live

And to whom I owe!

By Nat Scarcelli

THE HILLS AND MOUNTAINS

The hills and the mountains

Are just rebellious landscapes

Rising over the plains

Trying to get away

In order look over the 'fence'

For the greener landscapes.

They are deviant

Only to prove to the humans below

That it sucks to give in to gravity.

They escaped somehow

And by doing so,

Offered a wealth of scenery

Never possible before

To humans on the plains below.

It was never fair for only birds

To catch the breezes

And see the beauty

From their bird's-eye view.

A mountain, a hill,

Rebelliously

Rose higher than the winds

For us

(Tied to the ground

Unfairly by gravity)

To climb

To offer a wider world

And its beauty

From high above the ground,

Explains their defiance,

And rebellion.

By Nat Scarcelli

"I like this one I wrote (referring to the above poem). The only experience I have is Whiteface Mountain in the USA. A massive, rebellious landscape *daring* to rise and escape the 'below,' below. Lol.

Comments welcome.

Nat."

Image above of Dad with my eldest son at the 2024 high school graduation. My dad missed many events due to his state of mind at times. But when he did attend, it was always a sincere joy, and he made his love and pride known.

TIME

(Poem two of two of same title)

It went by fast

So slowly

I hardly noticed it.

And it is still moving fast slowly.

The clock shuts up

Most of the time

Its hands go around fast

So slowly

I could not keep track

Of each speeding hour

It never gonged past one hour

It went so fast

I could not hear them most of the time

Never got older.

So, it seemed.

We sailed often around the bay.

As quickly as the wild western winds

But never faster than a knot

And never got wet

The winds blew their heads off

And the boat never moved an inch

Or so it seemed.

At the end of summer,

We sighed it all went fast so slowly.

Today, the numbers rise high

On the birthday cakes

I forgot to count them

One by one

Through the chocolate cream

And half buried candles

With deleted numbers

Looking to the clock to remember,

But it stared back silently

Moving around its hands

Faster than a blender

Or as fast as jaguars

Moving in slow motion

Around my bed

As quickly as they could so slowly!

By Nat Scarcelli

IN ANY LANGUAGE

You know there are differences

In languages used to express thoughts
and feelings,

Either in a streams of consciousness

Or in meaningful navigations of the heart in broad daylight.

There are subtle differences almost deep like day and night.

One language or another could mean the difference between love and hate.

Or confuse you in fits of ignorance or enlightenment.

And mankind has uttered many examples of these, underlined or in quotations.

There are differences when you use English
or Italian

And worse if you know more of the multitude of languages out there.

I did not believe it, nor did I learn it, in the sentences expressed in both.

But the pitfalls were there for the inexperienced lover or the brand-new linguistic
graduate.

I called you one night on a dinner date in Italian, but you spoke to me angrily.

We ended up not eating an expensive meal at Giovanni's Restaurant.

We stared at each other in silence; I could not understand why you turned against
me.

And not one word of English or Italian came to
my rescue,

The relationship died as it was born near a plate of Veal and Eggplant

It silently grew cold and bitter like our conversation in either language did.

We could not speak either one, so both fell into the history books of linguistics.

There was nothing wrong with them upon deeper examination by experts.

We had fallen apart at once in silence near glasses of Evian and Veal Parmigiana

All the words of reconciliation in both dictionaries of Italy and Canada

Could not find the right ones to use in the witness of the waiter's patience.

Only a night of confusion stood out prominently flanked by; "It is finished and Finite!"

By Nat Scarcelli

THE MAJORITY DARKNESS

There is a majority of darkness everywhere.

Sometimes they call it shadows

Or just dark spaces Light forgot about.

Just like the nursing homes,

Filled up with pensions or waiting folks.

Both the same,

Where the black just covers the 'in-between',

Like enriched butter on slices of toast.

Or reaches far deep into money-lined savings.

If you're lucky, all matter that has a name,

Will get out of the way,

Should you navigate across it.

But not always does it pile up to the sides without blame

Or even under a generous bright-lighted guidance.

Sometimes you'll find your 'bump in the night'

That'll ruin your whole day or night,

Just the same.

By Nat Scarcelli
(Somewhere in Oshawa)

WANDERING THROUGH IT ALL

Illustrated by Nat Scarcelli:

A Self Portrait Wandering Outside

We'll wander for a little while in style

We'll search in vain, even under the carpet for missing files.

We're groomed like show horses

For big events.

We take photos to stop time.

But no one helps to break down fences

'They' let you wander

So that you think all along you're free.

But when your last breath is taken,

You realize among the thorns; you were never free.

Yes, you were never free,

At the point the curtain is drawn

And the precious children rise,

You'll never wander again to another dawn!

By Nat Scarcelli

THE DRYING OUT TIMES

Maybe the winds

Will drop off condolences

At my drying - out age

Just in time for Christmas.

The winds have their bites

They take them on the run.

There's no protection really,

No physical barrier.

No Christian mass.

Just like the fortune tellers predicted:

There'll be a great drying out time.

A time of utter aridity

Worse than in a desert.

A time for lotions

Coming out of the archives.

The youth will run around

With pockets of moisture

Oozing out

At gathering places in the night.

The drying out ones

Will make an appearance

But will eventually run out of the hall

For their lives.

By Nat Scarcelli

TODAY ONLY IS FOR SURE

I've been parked today

Fully awake

While the others

Raced from start to finish

On little trips

To end up parking

Far or near home.

We've done it all today

Safe and sound

Without a mishap

That we know about.

To earn a day alive,

For no one knows tomorrow,

Whether doing long

Or short trips,

There are no guarantees

For a starting gate tomorrow.

Or a place to park

Or a start- to- finish time to roll.

Only today was for sure!

By Nat Scarcelli

ON CREATIVITY

My poems run off the press

Out of fear.

No longer do they gather in clusters

Out of pride.

There is tension in the air.

I can feel the earth shaking and trembling

Out of fear too.

The lighted candle on the desktop

Is not too bright anymore.

The light has lost some of its hue.

You are all so far away from me

Maybe out of fear too?

I am not sure anymore like I was in a workplace

So, I sit alone and speculate,

Sometimes calm, sometimes short fused!

It has been a while since my poetry

Has rolled off the press.

And distributed to your address,

For your intimate consideration.

Creativity has ceased, the press run silent and broken in a mess!

By Nat Scarcelli

THANKSGIVING

Every day, especially today,

Become wonderful days

Quiet and reflective times.

To give thanks,

With acts of kindness

In words or rhymes,

It doesn't matter really how,

Even with signs or gestures.

As long as it comes from our inner being

No matter how small or big

To express a heartfelt thank you:

To the Creator.

To loved ones no longer with us,

But watching us from another dimension

Of existence.

And to those around us and active today,

Who have somehow performed acts of kindness,

And acts of favour and service

Along our journey through life,

And have saved us or changed us

Or brought us closer together

Or illuminated a pathway to a better life.

All who passed away or are alive today

Deserve thanks and recognition,

On a day like today.

For countless life changing kindnesses, favours and services,

Too many to mention,

It is a good day (and every day) to express gratitude-

Thank you.

CHECKING IN ON A WARRIOR

They were kind to me indeed

Checking in on me if an absence

Of one second at night

Passed without a greeting of essence.

But I was a young torch back when

And my light reached the stars,

And gave them a run for their light

All over the depth of the universe and to Mars.

But it is now August and some leaves are yellow

The greenery has lost its intensity

All the signs from the fashion world,

Hurry kids back to school from every corner of the city.

They have forgotten me and are letting me die

Alone, of course, without checking in on me,

With a kind hello or a jealous wink

So that I can wink back naturally.

By Nat Scarcelli

"Just a different variation of the same problem and a different manifestation of pains and aches...

but poetry is good for what ails me..."

Dad

HAPPY NEW YEAR FRIEND AND LOVE

It is one AM; I must have dozed off

On a slice of clock Just before midnight

And the magic stroke

Went unnoticed, dead as rock.

It happens when I'm alone

And the bottle of rye

Doesn't talk back to me

To remind me, to stay awake

Because I tipped it over and over

Until it got it mad at me.

It spilled its guts out for me in a glass,

But after the first time

It lost all meaning

As the evening progressed

It draped me in a cloth of loneliness,

Without pity, without meaning.

I wrote this poem to feel good,

And forget the bottle and sing Ault Lang Syne

Out of tune, but more sober

Just to wish you Happy New Year,

All night long on January First

For you as friend and love, while fairly sober!

By Nat Scarcelli at 1:15 AM January 1ˢ

LOVERS AT BAT

There were those days of work and sweat

When I came home lame and energy dead.

I could not wait until the midnight "lights out"

To wrap my limbs around you in bed.

We were young then and the leaves never changed colour

They just hanged on trees in the Fall like bats.

When they finally fell in glorious vermillion,

You gathered them in the evening, and you earned a turn at bat.

We made love late into the early morning

As the sweat dripped down in pools turning into wafers of salt.

Everything was creative and good results came into being like inventions.

As the suns, rise and set, day in and day out,

I must admit, I miss you a lot!

By Nat Scarcelli

JUST BEFORE FALLING ASLEEP

The buildings in the distance

Rise up against a troubled sky

With fragmented yellow lines

Of amber light.

The branches of the maple trees

Point with long narrow limbs

Drawing my attention

Where I am trying to sleep tonight.

One cannot help but be proud

Of this moment outside

Almost naked to the elements

To see nature's pulse beating strong and raw.

The night is an envelope

Holding a million thoughts and points of view.

They race across the mind into it,

And ready to be mailed out to the morning in awe.

By Nat Scarcelli

LIVE YOUR TIME

Live your time without thinking it's running out

Sleep in or sleep out without feeling guilty.

Or feeling that you're missing out; you're not.

There's so much happening, you want to be everywhere.

But you cannot be everywhere so accept your choices.

And understanding you are not missing out on anything in life.

Choose and do it.

Sleep in, take a nap, and do whatever you want

Don't save it for later; do it now.

Live your time without thinking it's running out.

Tomorrow will come around no matter what.

Even if you find yourself in Paris,

Or in New York at Carnegie Hall or on the streets

Just enjoy the time; you might not get the chance again!

By Nat Scarcelli